SOUS VIDE COOKBOOK

The best choice if you want to
have healthy and tasty food!

Table of Contents

Introduction

Regardless of whatever people might say, there is a hidden "Want" inside all of us to be able to create the most wonderful and magical meals that would help to win the heart of your family members and loved ones.

However, this is a feeble dream for some individuals who aren't blessed with the art of cooking and aren't able to manage enough time to hone their skill!

There was a time when even I was unable to cook an Omelet properly.

If you fall under that particular category, then you might be wondering now, is this the end of your culinary dreams?

Well of course not!

Thanks to constant evolutions in culinary technologies, we have amazing devices that not only make our cooking life easier but also makes it much more accessible so that anyone can cook wonderful meals, even without having an in-depth experience!

While it is true that there are some amazing appliances to consider such as the Air Fryer, Instant Pot, and Crock Pot etc., an undeniable fact is that the Sous Vide Appliances stand on a league of its own!

What is the best part about Sous Vide?

You will be able to cook perfect meal every single time, regardless of your culinary skill levels!

It might sound a little bit hard to believe, but it's true!

Before letting you go wild into the 100+ amazing recipes, which you can find in this book, I would like you to go through this introductory chapter to know more about your shiny Sous Vide device!

If you are already an experienced veteran, hope you will find some interesting things throughout the reading.

Alternatively, if you are an amateur and interested in learning the craft, the brief introductory chapter will give you all the necessary information required to help you fully grasp the science behind Sous Vide cooking.

Let's start with the core and explore the origin of Sous Vide first.

The history of Sous Vide

The origin of the technique of Sous Vide cooking dates to the mid-1970s when a very famous chef named Georges Pralus developed the technique with a hope of minimizing costly shrinkage and creating an optimal environment for cooking foie gras.

The news of this cooking technique spread like wildfire and was eventually picked up by another chef named Bruno Goussault.

Having understood the potentiality and delicacy of Sous Vide cooking, Bruno started to serve food prepared by Sous Vide to the first class guests of Air France.

The individuals who were lucky enough to taste the Sous Vide prepared meals were left completely mesmerized.

Once Bruno realized the true potential of this cooking technique, he went on to introduce it to the general audience.

Despite reaching a mass popularity, it still was a very expensive technique for normal people to afford and it took about 2 years of evolution before it completely broke the barriers and became one of the "Best" cooking technique ever made.

This reputation has also led to the creation of a more affordable device, using which people of every budget are now able to enjoy the delicacies of Sous Vide meals right from their own kitchen.

The following sections of the book will walk you through the concepts of Sous Vide.

The concept behind Sous Vide

Despite the popularity, the word "Sous Vide" still garners a lot of confusion amongst beginners.

Let me clarify this confusion first!

The word combination "Sous Vide" is actually a French one, which means "Under Vacuum".

Perhaps the major difference between Sous Vide cooking and other traditional forms of cooking is that in Sous Vide cooking you need to put your ingredients in a zip bag or a canning and seal them up to create a vacuum inside, which is later on submerged under carefully heated water, where the meal will be cooked to perfection.

This particular cooking method will only ask you to adjust the cooking temperature of the Sous Vide circulator.

Once you have done that, the water bath will slowly heat up and do the cooking for you.

It greatly simplifies the whole cooking process to a single factor, which allows anyone to master the technique in a moment and prepare an amazing meal in no time.

Some advantages of Using Sous Vide

Some of the core advantages of using Sous Vide are as follows:

- You will be able to capture the beautiful "essence" of gourmet flavors in your meal without being a master of the trade.
- Since you are not required to stare at the water bath, it saves a lot of time from your daily life.
- All of the natural juices and nutrients are perfectly stored in your sealed bags.
- The accurate cooking will allow you to cook all of your expensive cuts of meat to perfect every single time.

Health benefits of Sous Vide

The above-mentioned advantages are not the only good things that are going to come out from your Sous Vide experience, as there are a number of *health benefits* that you should be aware of as well.

- Sous Vide doesn't require you to add any additional fats or oil while cooking, which helps to make the prepared meal healthier. This allows your body to eventually lower down its cholesterol levels in the long run.
- Meals cooked by Souse Vide method are easier to digest as it helps to break down the collagen proteins into gelatin, which is easier for the body to adapt and absorb.
- Exposing ingredients to heat, oxygen, and water causes them to lose a lot of useful nutrients, which leads to over-carbonization of meats and

vitamin/antioxidant loss in vegetables. Sous Vide requires you to seal your ingredients in a vacuum-sealed pouch, as they don't come in contact with air or water, allowing them to preserve their nutrients.

How to prepare your kitchen for Sous Vide Cooking?

There is a misconception, which makes some people believe that Sous Vide cooking is rather expensive.

The truth is far from it though!

Using expensive equipment is an option, but it's not the only way!

You will still be able to get the job done using cheap and easy to find equipment that is just lying around the kitchen.

The only relatively "Expensive" device you need for Sous Vide cooking is the Sous Vide circulator itself.

Before you will know "Which" equipment you need for using let me introduce some of the famous Sous Vide circulators that are available in the market right now.

The Sous Vide Devices:

The Sous Vide devices are at the heart of modern Sous Vide cooking.

The core objective of these devices is to simply heat up water to a very specific temperature to precise water circulation and maintain the temperature all throughout the cooking session. The water circulation allows the heat to be distributed evenly and allows for even cooking.

If you have already purchased your first Sous Vide appliance, then you may skip this section, however, if this is your first time with the device, the section will be very helpful!

- **Anova Wifi Precision Cooker:**

This is the prime device when considering Sous Vide cooking and its launch pretty much had taken the world by storm. Asides from its cooking capabilities, It features mind-blowing functionalities such as Wi-Fi or Bluetooth connectivity that allows you to change the temperature and keep track of your cooking using your cell phone!

- **ChefSteps Joule:**

Sous Vide by ChefSteps has been known as the pioneer of the "Smart Kitchen" scene, and when they stepped into the market with their first Sous Vide machine, people were pleasantly surprised.

The device has a fantastic design and very compact size but packs the same level of power that can rival with any Sous Vide device of its double size.

This is the prime example of "Big Things Comes in Smaller Packages".

- **Gourmia Sous Vide Pod:**

The Gourmia Sous Vide Pod is perhaps the most affordable Sous Vide Circulator out there on the market at that moment. If you are looking for a device that does exactly what it is supposed to do, without sacrificing the "cool" looks, then it's what you need!

Besides from the Sous Vide appliances, a few other tools that you are going to need to include:

A reasonably large container:

The Sous Vide cooking technique will require you to heat up a water bath to a certain temperature as to submerge your sealed zip bag/container and cook the meal. A good quality 8-12 quart stockpot would perfectly do the trick. However, if you have the option, then go for a 12-quart square polycarbonate food storage container. Regardless, make sure to purchase a container that has the capacity to hold water heated up to 203 F.

Re-sealable bags and jars:

After a container, next, you will need re-sealable bags and jars.

For bags, you should go far heavy-duty re-sealable bag that is capable of sustaining temperatures of 195 F. Just make sure that the bags are marked "Freezer Safe" with a double seal.

When considering mason jars or cans, simply go for the ones with a tight lid.

Throughout the book, we will use the "Immersion" method to seal zip bags while the "Finger Tip Tight" technique for tightening cans.

Cast Iron Pan:

Having a good quality Cast Iron Pan is a good idea as some recipes will ask you to sear the meats after cooking.

Alternatively, you may also achieve a brown texture using a blowtorch as well.

How should you use the Sous Vide device?

Although some recipes will call for deviations in the process, the following are the basic steps that you need to know while using the Sous Vide Device during cooking.

Preparing: Once you have chosen your container, after attach your Immersion Circulator and fill the container with water. The height of the water should be just 1 inch above your device's minimum water level mark.

Dutch oven, plastic storage containers, stock pot and large saucepans are good options for Sous Vide cooking.

Choose temperature: When you have prepared your water bath, set the temperature of the device according to your recipe or ingredient.

Pre-heat water bath: Turn the device on and allow the water bath to reach the desired temperature, it should take about 20-30 minutes depending on your device.

Season and seal the meal: Season your food as instructed and vacuum seal it in zip bags or canning jars.

Submerge underwater: When the desired water level will be reached and you will seal your bags, submerge the food underwater and cover the container with a plastic wrap.

Wait until cooked: Wait until cooking process will complete.

Add finishing touches: When the cooking will be done, take the bag out and follow the rest of the recipe to add some finishing touches.

Understanding the sealing techniques

This is one of the more crucial aspects of Sous Vide cooking nowadays that seems to confuse many newcomers.

There are many expensive devices, which allow you to vacuum seal your zip bags in an instant! However, if you are on a tight budget, you may use techniques such as the "Immersion Method" to get the job done.

Water Immersion Method: This method is known as the Archimedes Principle Method. The steps are as follows:

- Put the ingredients in your bag first
- Gently start to submerge the bag under water, making sure to keep the upper part (the enclosure) above water
- As you have submerged the bag underwater, the pressure from the water will slowly push out any air that may be present in the zip bag.
- Submerge it just up to the zipper, and quickly lock up the zipper, making sure that no water has inserted the bag.

For canning jars, the Finger Tip Tight Technique is what you need to know.

Finger Tip Tight: This technique will require you carefully tighten the lid of your jars up until the point you experience the slightest amount of resistance. Make sure that you don't over tighten it as the air inside will not be able to escape.

The simplest way to do this - slowly keep tightening the lid and stop right at the moment when you first start to feel the slightest resistance.

Simple Sous Vide cooking time guidelines

For Meat

- Steak of about 1 ½ inch thickness takes a temperature of 129 F, and 2 hours for medium rare
- Hamburger - 130 F and 1 ½ h. for medium
- Beef Brisket - 135 F and 72 h. for medium, tender
- Beef Rib Roast - about 130 F and 1 ½ h. for medium
- Beef ribs - 158 F and 48 h. for medium
- Lamb Rack - 130 F and 2 ½ h. for medium
- Lamb Shoulder - 140 F and 24 h. hour for tender
- Pork Loin - 136 F and 2 h.
- Pork Belly - 158 F and 24 h.
- Pulled Pork Shoulder - 158 F and 24 h.
- Pulled Beef - 185 F and 24 h.
- Pork Ribs - 158 F and 24 h.

For Fish and Sea Food

- Salmon requires a temperature of 122 F and 20 min. (Medium rare, silky and moist)
- White Fish - 131 F and 30 min. (Silky and moist)
- Tuna Steak - 104 F and 1 h.
- Shrimp -135 F and 15 min.
- Calamari - 136 F and 1 ½ h.
- Octopus - 171 and 15 min.

- Lobster - 133 F and 15 min.
- Lobster Claws - 140 F and 15 min.
- Crab - 154 F and 45 min. (Steam on top of water)

For Poultry

- Chicken Breast requires a temperature of 140 F and 75 min. (for light meat)
- Chicken Thigh - 150 F and 2 h. (for dark meat)
- Duck Breast - 135 F 2 h. (for medium rare)
- Duck Leg - 167 F and 10 h. (tender, well done and shreds off very easily)

For Eggs

- Shell Poached requires a temperature of 147 F and 45 min. (for a uniform gooey texture)
- Shell Poached - 167 F and 13 min. (for a soft middle part with a harder white exterior)
- Hard Boiled - 170 F and 1 h.
- Scrambled - 167 F and 30 min.
- Gooey Yolks - 144 F and 1 h.

Chapter 1: Eggs and Appetizers

Crispy Bacon and Eggs

The most traditional English breakfast ever conceived! Make it with your Sous Vide cooker and pack yourself with enough energy to keep your running throughout the whole day.

Serving: 2

Prep Time: 10 minutes

Cook Time: 1 hour

Ingredients:

- 4 large sized egg yolks
- 2 slices of British style bacon rashers cut up into ½ inch by 3-inch slices
- 4 slices of crisp toasted bread

Directions:

1. Prepare your Sous Vide water bath by dipping your immersion cooker and raising the temperature to 143F
2. Gently place each of your egg yolks in the re-sealable bag and seal it up using immersion method
3. Submerge it underwater and let it cook for about 1 hour
4. In the meantime, fry your bacon slices until they are crisp

5. Drain them on a kitchen towel
6. Once the cooking of the eggs is done, serve by carefully removing the yolks from the bag and place them on top of your toast
7. Place a slice of bacon on top and serve!

Nutritional Info (Per Serving):

- Fat: 35g
- Protein: 32g
- Dietary Fiber: 2g
- Calories: 608

Egg Devils for Any Meal

Normal boiled eggs might get a bit boring after a while. Prepare these cute little-deviled eggs for you and your family members' pleasure.

Serving: 4

Prep Time: 15 minutes

Cook Time: 1 hour

Ingredients:

- 8 pieces of large eggs
- 3 tablespoon of mayonnaise
- 1 tablespoon of Dijon mustard
- Just a pinch of sugar
- Kosher salt as needed
- Ground black pepper as needed

Directions:

1. Prepare your Sous Vide water bath by dipping your immersion cooker and raising the temperature to 170F
2. Carefully use a slotted spoon and submerge the eggs underwater
3. Let them cook for 1 hour
4. Once the timer is off, use the slotted spoon to transfer the eggs to an ice water bath
5. Let them chill for about 20 minutes
6. Peel the eggs and cut them up in half lengthwise
7. Carefully remove the yolk and mash it with Dijon, mayonnaise, sugar
8. Season with some pepper and salt
9. Pip the mixture into the halves and serve!

Nutritional Info (Per Serving):

- Fat: 9g
- Protein: 6g
- Dietary Fiber: 3g
- Calories: 106

Honey Drizzled Baby Carrots

Carrots have a very high amount of nutritional goodness. These baby carrots are excellent as appetizers and the honey dressing makes the dish even more awesome.

Serving: 4

Prep Time: 5 minutes

Cook Time: 1 ¼ hours

Ingredients:

- 1 pound of baby carrots
- 4 tablespoon of butter
- 1 tablespoon of honey
- ¼ teaspoon of kosher salt
- ¼ teaspoon of ground cardamom

Directions:

1. Prepare the Sous Vide water bath by dipping the cooker and increasing the temperature to 185F
2. Add carrots, honey, butter, kosher salt, cardamom in a zip bag and seal using immersion method
3. Cook for 1 ¼ hours
4. Strain the glaze by passing it through a metal mesh and keep it on the side
5. Remove the carrots from the bag and pour the glaze over the carrots, serve and enjoy!

Nutritional Info (Per Serving)

- Fat: 1g
- Protein: 2g
- Dietary Fiber: 2g
- Calories: 174

Garlic Artichokes with Lemon

Artichokes are very common when it comes to choosing an appetizer. However, plain Artichokes might be too "Simple" for some of you, but when you mix it with a bit of garlic and drizzle of lemon it becomes amazingly delicious even for veggie haters.

Serving: 4

Prep Time: 30 minutes

Cook Time: 1 ½ hours

Ingredients:

- 4 tablespoon of freshly squeezed lemon juice
- 12 pieces of baby artichokes
- 4 tablespoon vegan butter
- 2 minced fresh garlic cloves
- 1 teaspoon of fresh lemon zest
- Kosher salt as needed
- Ground black pepper as needed
- Chopped up fresh parsley for serving

Directions:

1. Prepare the water bath by dipping the immersion cooker and raising the temperature to 180F
2. Take a large sized bowl and add cold water and 2 tablespoons of lemon juice
3. Peel and discard the outer tough layer of your artichoke and cut them up into quarters
4. Transfer them to a bowl of cold water and allow them to sit
5. Take a large sized skillet and place it over medium-high heat

6. Add butter and allow it to melt
7. Add garlic alongside 2 tablespoons of lemon juice and the zest
8. Remove the heat and season with a bit of pepper and salt
9. Allow it to cool for about 5 minutes
10. Drain the chokes form cold water and add them to a large-sized re-sealable bag
11. Add the butter mixture as well
12. Seal it up using immersion method and submerge it under water for about 1 ½ hour
13. Once the timer is off, transfer the chokes to a bowl and serve with a garnish of parsley

Nutritional Info (Per Serving):

- Fat: 8g
- Protein: 5g
- Dietary Fiber: 3g
- Calories: 200

Chapter 2: Vegan/Vegetarian

Germany's Potato Salad

This recipe is for potato Salad lovers. If you want something different, try this one! This special recipe originates from Germany, which uses Yukon potatoes to create an unforgettable experience.

Serving: 6

Prep Time: 30 minutes

Cook Time: 1 ½ hours

Ingredients:

- 1 ½ pound of Yukon potatoes, sliced up into ¾ inch pieces
- ½ a cup of chicken stock
- Salt as needed
- Pepper as needed
- 4 ounce of thick bacon cut up into ¼ inch thick strips
- ½ a cup of chopped onion
- 1/3 cup of apple cider vinegar
- 4 thinly sliced scallions

Directions:

1. Prepare your Sous Vide water bath by dipping your immersion cooker and raising the temperature to 185F

2. Take a heavy-duty re-sealable bag and add potatoes alongside the stock
3. Season with some salt and seal up the bag using immersion method
4. Submerge the bag underwater and let it cook for 1 and a 1/2 hours
5. Take a large sized non-stick skillet and place it over medium-high heat
6. Add bacon and cook for about 5-7 minutes
7. Transfer it to a paper towel-lined plate using a slotted spoon
8. Make sure to keep reserved fat
9. Return the skillet to medium-high heat and add onions
10. Cook them for a 1 minute
11. Once the cooking is done, remove the bag from the water and return the skillet to medium heat again
12. Add the bacon and add vinegar
13. Bring it to a simmer
14. Add the contents of the bag to the skillet and stir well to combine and allow the liquid to come to a simmer
15. Add scallions and toss well
16. Season with some pepper and salt
17. Serve warm!

Nutritional Info (Per Serving):

- Fat: 3g
- Protein: 7g
- Dietary Fiber: 2g
- Calories: 117

Momofuku Brussels

It's a desired recipe for many people who prefer to enjoy their weekend with a vegetable meal. Momofuku's special Brussels sprouts is a very attractive and delicious recipe, with equal parts of minty and sweet.

Serving: 2

Prep Time: 20 minutes

Cook Time: 40 minutes

Ingredients:

- 2 pounds of Brussels sprouts with stems trimmed and slice up in half
- 2 tablespoon of extra virgin olive oil
- ¼ tablespoon of extra virgin olive oil
- ¼ teaspoon of kosher salt
- ¼ cup of fish sauce
- 2 tablespoon of water
- 1 and a ½ tablespoon of granulated sugar
- 1 tablespoon of rice vinegar
- 1 and a ½ teaspoon of lime juice
- 12 pieces of thinly sliced Thai chills
- 1 small sized minced garlic clove
- Chopped up fresh mint
- Chopped up fresh cilantro

Directions:

1. Prepare your Sous Vide water bath by dipping your immersion cooker and raising the temperature to 183F

2. Take a heavy-duty re-sealable bag and add Brussels sprouts, salt, and olive oil
3. Seal it up using immersion method and cook underwater for 40 minutes
4. Take a small sized bowl and add fish sauce, sugar, water, rice vinegar, lime juice, garlic and chills to prepare the vinaigrette
5. Once the cooking is done, transfer the Brussels to an aluminum foil lined baking sheet
6. Heat up your broiler to high
7. Broil the Brussels in your broiler for about 5 minutes until they are just slightly charred
8. Transfer them to a medium-sized bowl and add the vinaigrette
9. Toss well
10. Sprinkle a bit of cilantro and mint
11. Serve!

Nutritional Info (Per Serving):

- Fat: 10g
- Protein: 3g
- Dietary Fiber: 2g
- Calories: 118

Long Green Beans in Tomato Sauce

This is a traditional Spanish dish, which combines the health factor of green beans and dredges them under a bucket load of tomato sauce. It's very simple and healthy recipe.

Serving: 4

Prep Time: 10 minutes

Cook Time: 3 hours

Ingredients:

- 1 pound of trimmed green beans
- 1 can of whole crushed tomatoes
- 1 thinly sliced onion
- 3 peeled and thinly sliced garlic clove
- Kosher salt as needed
- Extra virgin olive oil

Directions:

1. Prepare your Sous Vide water bath by dipping your immersion cooker and raising the temperature to 183F
2. Take a heavy duty zip bag and add tomatoes, green bean, garlic, and onion
3. Submerge underwater and cook for 3 hours
4. Remove the bag and transfer content to a large sized bowl
5. Season with salt and drizzle a bit of olive oil
6. Serve and enjoy!

Nutritional Info (Per Serving)

- Fat: 2g
- Protein: 4g
- Dietary Fiber: 2g
- Calories: 93

Hearty White Beans

White beans are very popular, as have useful elements for body system. You may prepare perfectly cooked white beans as a main dish and add any lovely recipe that you have as a side dish.

Serving: 8

Prep Time: 15 minutes

Cook Time: 3 hours

Ingredients:

- 1 cup of dried and soaked navy beans
- 1 cup of water
- ½ a cup of extra virgin olive oil
- 1 peeled carrot cut up into 1-inch dices
- 1 stalk of celery cut up into 1-inch dices
- 1 quartered shallot
- 4 cloves of crushed garlic
- 2 sprigs of fresh rosemary
- 2 pieces of bay leaves
- Kosher salt as needed
- Freshly ground black pepper as needed

Directions:

1. Prepare your Sous Vide water bath by dipping your immersion cooker and raising the temperature to 190F
2. Carefully drain and rinse your beans and add them to a heavy-duty zipper bag
3. Seal it up using immersion method and submerge it underwater

4. Let it cook for about 3 hours
5. Once done, taste the beans
6. If they are firm, then cook for another 1 hour, or cook for another hour and serve them on a bowl
7. Serve!

Nutritional Info (Per Serving)

- Fat: 3g
- Protein: 14g
- Dietary Fiber: 3g
- Calories: 152

Delicious Cardamom and Apricots

Halved apricots cooked with a drizzle of butter and spices, the perfect starter for anyone who enjoys the vegan root.

Serving: 4

Prep Time: 15 minutes

Cook Time: 1 hour

Ingredients:

- 1 pint of small and halved apricots
- 1 tablespoon of unsalted butter
- 1 teaspoon of cardamom seeds freshly ground
- ½ a teaspoon of ground ginger
- Just a pinch of smoked sea salt
- Chopped up fresh basil

Directions:

1. Prepare your Sous Vide water bath by increasing the temperature to a 180 degree Fahrenheit using an immersion cooker
2. Take a large sized heavy duty plastic bag and add butter, apricots, ginger, cardamom, salt and mix the whole mixture well
3. Seal up the bag using water displacement method and submerge it underwater
4. Let it cook for 1 hour and remove the bag once done
5. Take serving bowls and add the apricots to the bowl
6. Garnish with a bit of basil and serve!

Nutritional Info (Per Serving):

- Fat: 0g
- Protein: 1g
- Dietary Fiber: 3g
- Calories: 270

Chapter 3: Beef

Amazing Prime Rib

If you are a meat lover, you just can't ignore the juiciness of this EPIC prime rib. Just pack up the meat to you zip bag alongside the spices and you are good to go.

Serving: 12

Prep Time: 45 minutes

Cook Time: 6 hours

Ingredients:

- 3 pound of bone-in beef Ribeye roast
- Kosher salt
- 1 tablespoon of black peppercorn coarsely ground
- 1 tablespoon of green peppercorn coarsely ground
- 1 tablespoon of pink peppercorn coarsely ground
- 1 tablespoon of dried celery seeds
- 2 tablespoon of dried garlic powder
- 4 sprigs of rosemary
- 1 quart of beef stock
- 2 egg whites

Directions:

1. Season the beef with kosher salt and chill for 12 hours

2. Prepare the Sous Vide water bath by dipping the immersion cooker and waiting until the temperature has been raised to 132F
3. Transfer beef to zip bag and seal using immersion method
4. Cook for 6 hours
5. Preheat your oven to 425F and remove the beef, pat it dry
6. Take a bowl and whisk together peppercorn, celery seeds, garlic powder and rosemary
7. Brush the top of your cooked roast with egg white and season with the mixture and salt
8. Place the roast on a baking rack and roast for 10-15 minutes. Allow it to rest 10-15 minutes and carve
9. Take a large saucepan and add the cooking liquid from the bag, bring to a boil and simmer until half.
10. Carve the roast and serve with the juice

Nutritional Info (Per Serving):

- Fat: 40g
- Protein: 33g
- Dietary Fiber: 3g
- Calories: 504

Beef Willy Cheesesteak

Despite having a silly name, Philly "Willy" Cheesesteaks are sandwiches packed with a load of cheese and spices. In this case, with juicy beef also!

Serving: 4

Prep Time: 5 minutes

Cook Time: 1 hour + 2 minutes bake time

Ingredients:

- 1 thinly sliced bell pepper
- 1 thinly sliced yellow bell pepper
- ½ of a white onion thinly sliced up
- 2 tablespoon of extra virgin olive oil
- Kosher salt as needed
- Black pepper as needed
- 1 pound of thinly sliced cooked beef skirt steak
- 4 soft hoagie rolls
- 8 slices of Provolone cheese

Directions:

1. Prepare the Sous Vide water bath by dipping the immersion cooker and waiting until the temperature has been raised to 185F
2. Take a heavy duty zip bag and add yellow pepper, onion, olive oil, red pepper and season the mixture with salt and pepper
3. Seal using immersion method and cook for 1 hour
4. Take another bag and add steak, seal using immersion method, submerge and cook for 5 minutes

5. Pre-heat your oven to 400F
6. Slice the rolls in half and top them up with cheese
7. Transfer them to your oven and bake for 2 minutes
8. Add pepper, steak, and onion
9. Serve

Nutritional Info (Per Serving):

- Carbohydrate: 32g
- Protein: 43g
- Fat: 27g
- Calories: 531

Mesmerizing Beef Burgers

This one is for the burger aficionados. This is the prime example of a burger recipe, which lets you know that you don't have to visit KFC or McDonalds to get your burger fix. You can prepare premium quality beef burgers very easy using your Sous Vide cooker and light up your backyard party.

Serving: 4

Prep Time: 15 minutes

Cook Time: 1 hour + 1 minute sear time

Ingredients:

- 10 ounce of ground beef
- 2 hamburger buns
- 2 slices of American cheese
- Salt as needed
- Pepper as needed
- Condiments for topping
- Butter for toasting

Directions:

1. Prepare the Sous Vide water bath by dipping the immersion cooker and waiting until the temperature has been raised to 137F
2. Shape the beef into patties and season them with salt and pepper
3. Transfer to zip bag and seal using immersion method, cook for 1 hour
4. Toast the buns in butter warm cast iron pan
5. Once the burgers are cooked, transfer them to the pan and sear for 30 seconds per side

6. Place cheese on top and allow to melt
7. Assemble burger with topping and condiments
8. Serve!

Nutritional Info (Per Serving):

- Carbohydrate: 34g
- Protein: 11g
- Fat: 12g
- Calories: 287

Authentic Italian Sausage

«Mamma Mia» - are the first words that come to mind when considering Italian cuisine. While this recipe might not be the most elegant one of the Italian cuisine, but you have a good opportunity to prepare one of the most sought-after food in the world - "SAUSAGES"!

Serving: 4

Prep Time: 15 minutes

Cook Time: 1 hour + 3 minutes simmer time

Ingredients:

- 2 and a ½ cups of seedless red grapes with their stems removed
- 1 tablespoon of chopped fresh rosemary
- 2 tablespoon of butter
- 4 sweet Italian sausage
- 2 tablespoon of balsamic vinegar
- Salt as needed
- Ground black pepper as needed

Directions:

1. Prepare your Sous Vide water bath by dipping your immersion circulator and raising the temperature to 160F
2. Take a heavy duty zip bag and add butter, grapes, rosemary, sausages in a single layer
3. Seal using immersion method and cook for 1 hour underwater
4. Remove the sausages and transfer to plate
5. Take a small sized saucepan and add grapes alongside the liquid

41

6. Add balsamic vinegar and simmer for about 3 minutes over medium-high heat
7. Sear the sausages in the same saucepan for 3 minutes and serve with the grapes
8. Enjoy!

Nutritional Info (Per Serving):

- Fat: 51g
- Protein: 23g
- Dietary Fiber: 4g
- Calories: 661

Party Beef Hot Dogs

Now when you know how to make Sausages, let me show you how to prepare amazing hot dogs. Just make sure "NOT" to add too much mustard or ketchup.

Serving: 4

Prep Time: 5 minutes

Cook Time: 1 hour

Ingredients:

- 8 hot dogs
- 8 hot dog buns
- Mustard
- Ketchup

Directions:

1. Prepare the Sous Vide water bath by dipping the immersion cooker and waiting until the temperature has been raised to 140F
2. Add the hot dogs to your zip bag and seal using immersion method
3. Submerge and cook for 60 minutes
4. Serve by adding the hot dogs in the bun and dressing with a bit of mustard and ketchup
5. Enjoy!

Nutritional Info (Per Serving):

- Fat: 10g
- Protein: 6g
- Dietary Fiber: 3g
- Calories: 126

Original Soy Garlic Tri-Tip

Tri-Tips are perhaps one of the most misunderstood beef cut. Just to make things clear, a Tri-Top is a triangular cut from the bottom of sirloin sub of the beef. This recipe allows you to prepare an awesome Tri-Tip steak, which is dressed with soy and garlic. Delicious!

Serving: 4

Prep Time: 5 minutes

Cook Time: 2 hours + 2 minutes sear time

Ingredients:

- 2 pound of Tri-Tip Steak Roast
- Salt as needed
- Pepper as needed
- 2 tablespoon of soy sauce
- 6 cloves of pre-roasted garlic, crushed

Directions:

1. Prepare your Sous Vide water bath and increase the temperature to 129F
2. Season the tri-tip well with pepper and salt
3. Add the meat to your zip bag alongside soy sauce and crushed garlic cloves
4. Seal the bag using immersion method
5. Submerge and cook for 10 minutes
6. Take a cast iron skillet and place it over medium heat
7. Sear the meat for 1 minute per side until browned
8. Slice and serve!

Nutritional Info (Per Serving):

- Carbohydrate: 10g
- Protein: 31g
- Fat: 23g
- Calories: 384

Chapter 4: Pork

Cider and Rosemary Pork with Caramel Sauce

Unlike most other recipes, this one has a bit of bone inside. Nevertheless, the caramel sauce and seasoning of rosemary and cider create a blissful flavor that melts in your mouth.

Serving: 1

Prep Time: 25 minutes

Cook Time: 46 minutes

Ingredients:

- 1 pound of bone-in, double cut pork chop
- 1 sprig of chopped rosemary
- Kosher salt as needed
- Ground black pepper as needed
- 1 chopped garlic clove
- 1 cup of divided hard cider
- 1 tablespoon of vegetable oil
- 1 tablespoon of dark brown sugar
- Sautéed cabbage as needed
- Sautéed apples as needed

Directions:

1. Prepare the Sous Vide water bath by submerging the cooker and increasing the temperature to 140F
2. Season the pork chop with salt and pepper

3. Rub the chop with rosemary and garlic
4. Take a heavy-duty re-sealable bag and add ½ cup of hard cider and the pork chop
5. Seal it using the immersion method
6. Submerge it underwater and cook for 4 minutes
7. Once ready, remove the bag and pat the chops dry using a kitchen towel
8. Take a cast iron skillet and add veggie oil, swirl it gently
9. Add the chops to the skillet and sear until golden brown (for 45 seconds per side)
10. Allow it to rest for about 5 minutes
11. Pour the sauce into the skillet from the bag and add1/2 a cup of cider
12. Add sugar and keep stirring until sugar has melted
13. Simmer for 1 minute and pour the sauce over the pork chop
14. Serve with cabbage and apple

Nutritional Info (Per Serving):

- Carbohydrate: 1g
- Protein: 35g
- Fat: 26g
- Calories: 382

Coconut Boneless Pork Ribs

Pork ribs are generally delicious all-around. This recipe takes the thing up a notch and adds the flavor of coconut milk to the mix, giving a wonderful mixture of juicy pork meat and coconut milk.

Serving: 4

Prep Time: 30 minutes

Cook Time: 8 hours + 20 minutes simmer time

Ingredients:

- 1/3 cup unsweetened coconut milk
- 2 tablespoons peanut butter
- 2 tablespoons soy sauce
- 2 tablespoons light brown sugar
- 2 tablespoons dry white wine
- 2-inch fresh lemongrass
- 1 tablespoon Sriracha
- 1 inch peeled fresh ginger
- 2 cloves garlic
- 2 teaspoons sesame oil
- 12 oz. boneless country style pork ribs
- Chopped up fresh cilantro and steamed basmati rice for serving

Directions:

1. Prepare your Sous Vide water bath by adding the immersion circulator and increasing the temperature to 134F
2. Add coconut milk, peanut butter, brown sugar, soy sauce, wine, lemongrass, ginger, garlic, Sriracha,

garlic and sesame oil to a blender and blend until smooth

3. Add ribs to a zip bag alongside the sauce and seal using immersion method
4. Cook for 8 hours
5. Remove the bag and remove the ribs from the bag, transfer to plate.
6. Pour the bag contents into a large skillet and place it over medium-high heat, bring to a boil and lower heat to medium-low. Simmer for 10-15 minutes.
7. Add ribs to the sauce and turn well to coat it.
8. Simmer for 5 minutes.
9. Garnish with cilantro and serve with rice!

Nutritional Info (Per Serving):

- Carbohydrate: 24g
- Protein: 53g
- Fat: 59g
- Calories: 840

Delicious Bacon and Pearl Onions

Everybody loves bacon, and the pearl onions here will only add another dimension of flavor to the good old recipe.

Serving: 4

Prep Time: 10 minutes

Cook Time: 1 ½ hour

Ingredients:

- 1 pound of peeled pearl onions
- 1 sliced crumbled and cooked bacon
- 1 stem of thyme with only leaves

Directions:

1. Prepare the water bath by dipping the immersion cooker and raising the temperature to 185 F
2. Take a zip bag and add bacon, thyme, pearl, onion, and seal using immersion method
3. Submerge the bag and cook for 90 minutes
4. Remove the bag and strain the liquid
5. Serve the bacon with the strained sauce and enjoy!

Nutritional Info (Per Serving):

- Carbohydrate: 25g
- Protein: 16g
- Fat: 30g
- Calories: 438

Japanese Pork Cutlets

These Pork cutlets are prepared by a classical Japanese technique. In addition, these cutlets are slightly crispy and offer a warm and subtle texture for your eating pleasure.

Serving: 6

Prep Time: 15 minutes

Cook Time: 1 hour

Ingredients:

- 3 pork loin chops
- Salt as needed
- Pepper as needed 1 cup of flour
- 2 pieces of eggs

Directions:

1. Prepare the Sous Vide water bath by dipping the immersion cooker and waiting until the temperature has been raised to 140F
2. Make tiny slits on the loin body and trim excess fat
3. Season them with pepper and salt
4. Transfer them to zip bag and seal using immersion method and submerge, cook for 1 hour
5. Remove the loin chops from the bag and pat them dry
6. Dredge the loin in flour, egg and finally the panko crumbs
7. Heat up oil to 450 F and fry for 1 minute
8. Place them on a cooling rack and slice it up
9. Serve with top steamed rice and veggies
10. Enjoy!

Nutritional Info (Per Serving):

- Carbohydrate: 45g
- Protein: 8g
- Fat: 7g
- Calories: 260

Lemongrass Pork Chops

Lemongrass is usually reserved for Thai dishes such as Green Curry or Thai soups. It combines the essence of Thai with a very traditional pork chop recipe and gives something amazing in the process.

Serving: 2

Prep Time: 30 minutes

Cook Time: 2 hours

Ingredients:

- 2 tablespoon of coconut oil
- 1 stalk of sliced lemon grass
- 1 tablespoon of minced shallot
- 1 tablespoon of soy sauce
- 1 tablespoon of mirin
- 1 tablespoon of rice wine vinegar
- 1 tablespoon of light brown sugar
- 1 teaspoon of minced fresh ginger
- 1 teaspoon of fish sauce
- 1 teaspoon of kosher salt
- 2 bone-in pork rib chops

Directions:

1. Prepare the Sous Vide water bath by dipping the immersion cooker and waiting until the temperature has been raised to 140F
2. Take a food processor and add 1 tablespoon of coconut oil, lemongrass, soy sauce, shallot, mirin, vinegar, brown sugar, garlic, ginger, fish sauce and salt

3. Process the whole mixture for 1 minute
4. Transfer the pork chops to zip bag alongside the lemongrass mix, seal using immersion method
5. Cook for about 2 hours
6. Remove the bag and remove the pork chops, pat them dry
7. Heat up a grill to high heat and sear the chops until browned
8. Rest for 2-3 minutes and serve!

Nutritional Info (Per Serving):

- Carbohydrate: 12g
- Protein: 26g
- Fat: 12g
- Calories: 262

Chapter 5: Poultry

Easy Turkey Legs

Turkeys are not just reserved for Thanksgiving. If you want Turkey legs, follow this recipe and you should have a perfectly cooked one with no hassle at all.

Serving: 4

Prep Time: 15 minutes

Cook Time: 14 hours

Ingredients:

- 2 pieces of turkey legs
- 1 tablespoon of extra virgin olive oil
- 1 tablespoon of garlic salt
- 1 teaspoon of freshly ground black pepper
- 3 sprigs of thyme

Directions:

1. Prepare your Sous Vide water bath by dipping your immersion circulator and raising the temperature to 145F
2. Season the turkey carefully with garlic salt and pepper
3. Transfer to a heavy duty zip bag and add thyme
4. Seal using immersion method and submerge water
5. Cook for 14 hours, making sure to keep the container covered with plastic wrap
6. Remove and pat the legs dry with kitchen towel
7. Take an iron skillet and place it over high heat

8. Remove the legs and rub with olive oil, transfer to the pan and sear for 2 and a ½ minutes
9. Serve and enjoy!

Nutritional Info (Per Serving):

- Fat: 47g
- Protein: 87g
- Dietary Fiber: 3g
- Calories: 925

Simple Chicken Breast

This recipe offers you the opportunity to cook a chicken and eat it right from the bag without any further processing.

Serving: 2

Prep Time: 5 minutes

Cook Time: 1 or 2 hours

Ingredients:

- Boneless chicken breast
- Salt as needed
- Pepper as needed
- Garlic powder as needed

Directions:

1. Prepare your Sous Vide water bath by dipping your immersion circulator and raising the temperature to 150F
2. Drain your chicken breast carefully and pat it dry using a kitchen towel
3. Season the breast with pepper, garlic powder, and salt
4. Add the breast to a heavy-duty re-sealable bag and zip it up using the immersion method
5. Submerge it underwater and let it cook for about 2 hours if the breast is of 2-inch thickness and 1 hour for a breast of 1-inch thickness
6. Serve!

Nutritional Info (Per Serving):

- Fat: 17g
- Protein: 18g
- Dietary Fiber: 2g
- Calories: 232

Majestic Turkey Breast

The legs aren't the only delicious parts of Turkey! If you want to deviate from the common trend and try out soft and tender Turkey breast, then go on with this recipe and you should have a yummy turkey breast ready at your platter.

Serving: 6

Prep Time: 15 minutes

Cook Time: 3 hours + 5 minutes sear time

Ingredients:

- 1 boneless turkey breast half with skin on
- 1 tablespoon of extra virgin olive oil
- 1 tablespoon of garlic salt
- 1 teaspoon of freshly ground black pepper

Directions:

1. Prepare your Sous Vide water bath by dipping your immersion cooker and raising the temperature to 145F
2. Season the turkey with garlic salt and pepper
3. Transfer the breast to a heavy-duty re-sealable zip bag alongside olive oil
4. Seal using immersion method and cook for 3 hours
5. Remove the bag and pat it dry using kitchen towel
6. Take an iron skillet and place it over high heat
7. Add turkey breast and sear with the skin side facing down for 5 minutes
8. Serve and enjoy!

Nutritional Info (Per Serving):

- Fat: 18g
- Protein: 41g
- Dietary Fiber: 2g
- Calories: 338

Singaporean Chicken Wings

Who doesn't love chicken wings? We all do! However, if you are looking for something a bit special, then try out this Singaporean chicken wings recipe, with equal sweet and spicy parts.

Serving: 2

Prep Time: 15 minutes

Cook Time: 2 hours and 5 minutes

Ingredients:

- ¾ teaspoon of soy sauce
- ¾ teaspoon of Chinese rice wine
- ¾ teaspoon of honey
- ¼ teaspoon of five-spice
- 2 whole chicken wings
- ½ an inch of fresh ginger
- 1 clove of smashed garlic
- Sliced scallions for serving

Directions:

1. Prepare your Sous Vide water bath by dipping your immersion cooker and raising the temperature to 160F
2. Take a bowl and add soy sauce, honey, rice wine, five spice and mix
3. Transfer the chicken wings, garlic, and ginger to zip bag
4. Seal using immersion method and cook for 2 hours
5. Heat up the broiler to high and line up a broil-safe baking sheet with aluminum foil

6. Remove the wings and transfer to broiling pan, broil for 3-5 minutes
7. Transfer the serving platter and sprinkle sliced scallions
8. Enjoy!

Nutritional Info (Per Serving):

- Carbohydrate: 11g
- Protein: 21g
- Fat: 18g
- Calories: 402

Sweet Chili Chicken

This recipe falls more on the side of Thai/Chai cuisine, so if you are into that type of meals, or if you like the sweet chicken dish in general, then go for this one. This recipe provides the perfect blend of sweetness and chili to create a mouthwatering medley of flavors.

Serving: 2

Prep Time: 30 minutes

Cook Time: 2 hours

Ingredients:

- 4 chicken thigh
- 2 tablespoon of olive oil
- Salt as needed
- Pepper as needed
- 1 crushed garlic clove
- 3 tablespoon of fish sauce
- ¼ cup of lime juice
- 1 tablespoon of palm sugar
- 3 tablespoon of chopped Thai basil
- 3 tablespoon of chopped cilantro
- 2 chopped up red chilies (deseeded)
- 1 tablespoon of sweet chili sauce

Directions:

1. Carefully prepare your water bath using your Sous Vide immersion cooker and pre-heating it to a temperature of 150F
2. Cover the breast with cling film and chill them for a while

3. Transfer them to your zip bag with olive oil, salt, pepper and oil and seal using immersion method and cook for 2 hours
4. Once done, heat up a pan with vegetable oil and chop up the chicken skin into 4-5 pieces
5. Dip them in the veggie oil and cook until crispy
6. Combine all the dressing ingredients in a bowl and keep it on the side
7. Sprinkle salt on top and serve with the sauce

Nutritional Info (Per Serving):

- Carbohydrate: 9g
- Protein: 46g
- Fat: 54g
- Calories: 721

Chapter 6: Fish and seafood

Mesmerizing Shrimp

Simplicity is the main "Ingredient" in this shrimp recipe. If you have a craving for shrimp, then simply use this recipe to create a batch of amazing cooked shrimp within just 30 minutes.

Serving: 4

Prep Time: 10 minutes

Cook Time: 24 minutes

Ingredients:

- 1 chopped red onion
- Juice of 2 limes
- 1 teaspoon of extra virgin olive oil
- ¼ teaspoon of sea salt
- 1/8 teaspoon of white pepper
- 1 pound of raw shrimp, peeled and divided
- 1 diced tomato
- 1 diced avocado
- 1 seeded and diced jalapeno
- 1 tablespoon of chopped cilantro

Directions:

1. Prepare your Sous Vide water bath by dipping your immersion cooker and increasing the temperature to 148F
2. Add lime juice, red onion, sea salt, pepper, olive oil, white pepper, shrimp to a heavy duty zip bag

3. Seal using immersion method and cook for 24 minutes
4. Remove the bag and chill in ice bath for 10 minutes
5. Take a large sized bowl and add tomato, avocado, cilantro, and jalapeno
6. Mix well and top up the salad with the shrimp
7. Enjoy!

Nutritional Info (Per Serving):

- Fat: 19g
- Protein: 10g
- Dietary Fiber: 0g
- Calories: 220

Salmon with Hollandaise Sauce

Gently cooked Salmon bathed in delicious and homemade "Healthy" hollandaise sauce. It's one of the best decisions for wine evening.

Serving: 4

Prep Time: 5 minutes + 30 minutes chill time

Cook Time: 1 hour and 15 min

Ingredients:

- 2 salmon fillets
- Salt as needed

Hollandaise Sauce

- 4 tablespoon of butter
- 1 egg yolk
- 1 teaspoon of lemon juice
- 1 teaspoon of water
- ½ of a diced shallots
- Just a pinch of cayenne
- Salt as needed

Directions:

1. Prepare your salmon by rubbing it with salt
2. Let it chill in your fridge for 30 minutes
3. Prepare your water bath by heating it up to 148F
4. Take a large-sized Sous Vide plastic bag and add the ingredients for the sauce
5. Seal it up using immersion method
6. Submerge it underwater and cook for 45 minutes

7. Once the sauce is done, lower the temperature of your bath to the temperature required for your salmon
8. Add the salmon to another re-sealable bag and add the salmon, seal it well using immersion method
9. Cook it for 30 minutes under water
10. Remove the sauce from your water bath and pour it in a blender
11. Blend it well until a light yellow texture appears
12. Remove the Salmon from your bath and pat them dry
13. Sear if needed and serve with the hollandaise sauce

Nutritional Info (Per Serving):

- Fat: 28g
- Protein: 33g
- Dietary Fiber: 2g
- Calories: 418

Scallop, Curry and Sous Vide Magic

Incredibly basic curry dish that comes with a very versatile dressing, which altogether makes a magical Scallops to prepare with your Sous Vide circulator!

Serving: 2

Prep Time: 15 minutes

Cook Time: 1 hour

Ingredient:

- 2 tablespoon of yellow curry powder
- 1 tablespoon of tomato paste
- ½ a cup of coconut cream
- 1 teaspoon of chili garlic sauce
- 1 teaspoon of chicken base
- 1 tablespoon of freshly squeezed lime juice
- 6 large sized sea scallops
- Cooked basmati rice
- Chopped up fresh cilantro

Directions:

1. Prepare your Sous Vide water bath by dipping your immersion cooker and raising the temperature to 134F
2. Take a medium-sized bowl and add coconut cream, tomato paste, curry powder, lime juice, chicken baste, chili-garlic sauce and mix well
3. Add the mix to a heavy duty zip bag alongside the scallops and seal using immersion method

4. Cook for 1 hour and once the cooking is done, transfer the contents to a serving bowl
5. Serve the scallops on top Basmati rice and a bit of chopped fresh cilantro
6. Enjoy!

Nutritional Info (Per Serving):

- Fat: 8g
- Protein: 10g
- Dietary Fiber: 3g
- Calories: 239

Chapter 7: Sauces

Dulce De Leche

A sweet serving from Argentina, which is condensed milk that can be eaten alone, used to fill cakes or even served with bananas. The possibilities are endless here.

Serving: 4

Prep Time: 5 minutes

Cook Time: 12 hours

Ingredients:

- 1 can of 12 ounces condensed milk

Directions:

1. Prepare your Sous Vide water bath to a temperature of 185F
2. Seal the sweetened condensed milk in a canning jar
3. Submerge and cook for 12 hours
4. Serve immediately!

Nutritional Info (Per Serving):

- Carbohydrate: 29g
- Protein: 22g
- Fat: 13g
- Calories: 320

Cauliflower Alfredo

This one for the vegetarians and vegans, who love Alfredo Sauce and are looking for something to satisfy their diet regime. This Cauliflower Alfredo is the perfect companion for your zucchini pasta or any similar dish.

Serving: 4

Prep Time: 5 minutes

Cook Time: 2 hours

Ingredients:

- 2 cups of chopped cauliflower florets
- 2 crushed garlic cloves
- 2 tablespoon of butter
- ½ a cup of chicken stock
- 2 tablespoon of milk
- Salt as needed
- Pepper as needed

Directions:

1. Prepare your Sous Vide water bath to a temperature of 181F
2. Add the contents to a zip bag and seal using immersion method
3. Cook for 2 hours and transfer the contents to a food processor
4. Puree and serve!

Nutritional Info (Per Serving):

- Carbohydrate: 29g
- Protein: 22g
- Fat: 13g
- Calories: 320

Indian Mango Sauce

Also known as Mango "Chutney" in India, this blend of mango and other spices will give you a very delicate mango sauce that comes with a chunky "Melt in your mouth" texture.

Serving: 4

Prep Time: 10 minutes

Cook Time: 1 hour

Ingredients:

- 1 large sized ripe mango, peeled and cut up into small dices
- ¼ cup of Granny Smith Apple, cored, peeled and cut up into small dice
- ¼ of finely chopped red onion
- ¼ cup of packed light brown sugar
- 1 and ½ tablespoon of malt vinegar
- 1 finely chopped chile
- ½ a teaspoon of grated fresh ginger
- Pinch of salt

Directions:

1. Prepare your Sous Vide water bath to a temperature of 180F
2. Add everything to a zip bag
3. Seal using immersion method
4. Cook for 1 hour
5. Serve or store in container for up to 2 weeks

Nutritional Info (Per Serving):

- Carbohydrate: 11g
- Protein: 3g
- Fat: 17g
- Calories: 196

Chapter 8: Drinks

Limoncello

A very distinguishable and refreshing lemon drink that easily stands out from the crowd due to its authentic flavor, which gives you the genuine taste of biting a lemon "Without" actually eating one.

Serving: 12

Prep Time: 15 minutes

Cook Time: 2 hours

Ingredients:

- 10 organic fresh lemons
- 4 cups of vodka
- 4 cups of water
- 1 ½ cups of superfine sugar

Directions:

1. Prepare your Sous Vide water bath by dipping your immersion cooker and raising the temperature to 135F
2. Wash the lemons well using hot water and pat them dry with a kitchen towel
3. Take vegetable peeler and remove the zest by cutting them into strips
4. Save the lemon for later use
5. Add zest to a zip bag alongside vodka and seal using immersion method
6. Cook for 2 hours

7. Take a saucepan and place it over medium-high heat and add water and sugar, stir until dissolved
8. Strain the contents of the bag through a metal mesh into a bowl and stir in the syrup
9. Transfer Limoncello to bottles and serve in glass
10. Enjoy!

Nutritional Info (Per Serving):

- Fat: 0g
- Protein: 0g
- Dietary Fiber: 2g
- Calories: 262

Delicious Coffee Liquor

The people of New Hampshire used this recipe for more than 70 years. Just a small amount of this beverage has as much power as in 5 pints of coffee. Highly recommended for coffee buffs and enthusiasts.

Serving: 20

Prep Time: 10 minutes

Cook Time: 3 hours

Ingredients:

- 1 bottle of vodka
- 32 ounce of strong black coffee
- 2 cups of granulated sugar
- ½ a cup of coffee beans
- 2 split vanilla beans

Directions:

1. Prepare your Sous Vide water bath by dipping your immersion cooker and raising the temperature to 145F
2. Add the listed ingredients to your zip bag and seal using immersion method
3. Cook for 3 hours under water and pass the contents through a metal mesh
4. Allow it to cool and serve!

Nutritional Info (Per Serving):

- Fat: 32g
- Protein: 6g
- Dietary Fiber: 3g
- Calories: 451

Lemon Meyer

Meyer Lemons are unique in the sense that they have a very interesting flavor, which acts as somewhat of a hybrid between a lemon and an orange. This drink will simply give you the best of both worlds.

Serving: 6

Prep Time: 15 minutes

Cook Time: 2 hours

Ingredients:

- 1 cup of vodka
- 1 cup of granulated sugar
- 1 cup of freshly squeezed Meyer lemon
- Zest of 3 Meyer lemon

Directions:

1. Prepare your Sous Vide water bath by dipping your immersion cooker and raising the temperature to 135F
2. Take a re-sealable bag and add all of the listed ingredients and seal it up using immersion method
3. Submerge and cook for about 2 hours
4. Once the cooking is done, strain the mixture through a fine metal mesh strainer into a medium-sized bowl
5. Chill it overnight and serve!

Nutritional Info (Per Serving):

- Fat: 1g
- Protein: 1g
- Dietary Fiber: 2g
- Calories: 374

Vanilla Bean and Bourbon Soda

Bourbon Soda topped off with the essence of vanilla and the sweetness of sugar. Prepare this drink if you are looking for something to surprise your friends and make no compromises in the process.

Serving: 3

Prep Time: 10 minutes

Cook Time: 2 hours

Ingredients:

- 1 cup of granulated sugar
- ½ a cup of water
- ½ a cup of bourbon
- 6 split vanilla beans
- Club soda for serving
- Orange wedges for serving

Directions:

1. Prepare your Sous Vide water bath by dipping your immersion cooker and raising the temperature to 135F
2. Take a re-sealable bag and add sugar, water, vanilla, and bourbon and seal it up using immersion method
3. Submerge and cook for about 2 hours
4. Once the cooking is done, strain the mixture through a fine metal mesh strainer into a medium-sized bowl
5. Chill it overnight

6. Serve with one part syrup, two-part soda in rocks glass over ice
7. Garnish with a piece of an orange wedge and enjoy!

Nutritional Info (Per Serving):

- Fat: 7g
- Protein: 1g
- Dietary Fiber: 2g
- Calories: 160

10 Minutes Ginger Gin

Are you looking for a quick and easy cold drink to satisfy summer thirst? Create this concoction of vodka and berries for a delicate and extremely refreshing Sous Vide "Ginger Gin"!

Serving: 2

Prep Time: 5 minutes + 15 minutes chill time

Cook Time: 10 minutes

Ingredients:

- 3 ounce of vodka
- 10 pieces of coriander seeds
- 8 pieces of juniper berries
- 2 pieces of dried lavender
- 5 whole black peppercorns
- 2 whole pods
- 1 piece of bay leaf
- Tonic water as needed
- Lime wedges for serving

Directions:

1. Prepare your Sous Vide water bath by dipping your immersion cooker and raising the temperature to 176F
2. Take a large sized re-sealable bag and add vodka, juniper, coriander, cardamom, peppercorns, bay leaf, lavender
3. Seal it up using immersion method and submerge it underwater
4. Let it cook for 10 minutes

5. Once done, strain the mixture through a fine metal mesh into a bowl and chill for 15 minutes
6. Serve with a mixture of tonic water and some lime wedge

Nutritional Info (Per Serving):

- Fat: 0g
- Protein: 0g
- Dietary Fiber: 2g
- Calories: 112

Chapter 9: Desserts

Superb Vanilla Pudding

Very easy pudding that will help to create a perfect end of the dinner. This dessert is so tasty, that even the smallest members of your family will like it.

Serving: 6

Prep Time: 15 minutes

Cook Time: 45 minutes

Ingredients:

- 1 cup of whole milk
- 1 cup of heavy cream
- ½ a cup of ultrafine sugar
- 3 large pieces of egg (additional 2 egg yolks)
- 3 tablespoon of cornstarch
- 1 tablespoon of vanilla extract
- Pinch of kosher salt

Directions:

1. Prepare the Sous Vide water bath and dip the immersion cooker and raise the temperature to 180F
2. Take a blender and add the ingredients to the blender and puree for 30 seconds until you have a frothy mix
3. Transfer the mixture to a re-sealable bag and seal it up using immersion method

4. Submerge the bag underwater and cook for 45 minutes
5. Shake the bag about half way through to prevent the formation of clump
6. Once cooked, remove the bag and transfer it to the blender once more
7. Puree again until smooth
8. Transfer it to a bowl and allow it to chill
9. Serve with a garnish of strawberries or your favorite topping

Nutritional Info (Per Serving):

- Fat: 25g
- Protein: 19g
- Dietary Fiber: 2g
- Calories: 421

Banana Bread Meal

A very healthy dessert that kids will love and adults will enjoy! The moistness of this bread meal will give you the best tasting Sous Vide banana bread, which your family members will love to the core!

Serving: 12

Prep Time: 30 minutes

Cook Time: 2 hours

Ingredients:

- ½ a cup of butter
- ½ a cup of brown sugar
- ½ a cup of white sugar
- 2 pieces of eggs
- 1 teaspoon of vanilla
- 1 teaspoon of salt
- 3 tablespoon of milk
- 3 ripe bananas mashed up
- 1/2 a teaspoon of baking soda
- 2 cups of all-purpose flour
- ½ a cup of nuts

Directions:

1. Set up your Sous Vide immersion circulator to a temperature of 170F and prepare your water bath
2. Add butter, white sugar, brown sugar to a warm skillet and mix well
3. Once the butter and sugar mixture cools, add the milk, egg, vanilla, salt and stir well until fully dissolved

4. Add flour, bananas, and soda and mix well
5. Cast the mixture into pre-greased 4-ounce mason jars and lightly seal the lid
6. Cook for 2 hours
7. Take it out and serve!

Nutritional Info (Per Serving):

- Fat: 25g
- Protein: 19g
- Dietary Fiber: 2g
- Calories: 421

Pumpkin Crème Brule

Taste this delicious Crème Brule, cooked to perfection and tinted with flavors of pumpkin. An amazing and delightful twist on the age-old recipe.

Serving: 6

Prep Time: 10 minutes

Cook Time: 1 hour 10 minutes

Ingredients:

- 1 cup of milk
- 1 cup of heavy whipping cream
- 3 whole eggs
- 3 pieces of egg yolks
- ½ a cup of pumpkin puree
- ¼ cup of maple syrup
- ½ a teaspoon of pumpkin spice
- Just a pinch of salt
- Granulated sugar

Directions:

1. Set up your Sous Vide immersion circulator to a temperature of 167F and prepare your water bath
2. Take a bowl and milk, heavy cream, 3 whole eggs, 3 egg yolks, ½ a cup of pumpkin puree, ¼ cup of maple syrup, ½ a teaspoon of pumpkin spice and pinch a kosher salt
3. Mix well and keep whisking until it is combined and smooth
4. Pour the mixture into 6 – 4-ounce mason jars
5. Place the lid loosely and cook for 1 hour

6. Allow them to chill
7. Spread a thin layer of sugar on top of the custard and caramelize with a blow torch
8. Serve!

Nutritional Info (Per Serving):

- Fat: 25g
- Protein: 19g
- Dietary Fiber: 2g
- Calories: 421

Delicious Banana Oatmeal

Oatmeal is accepted all around the world to be one of the healthiest breakfast for everyone. With this recipe, you will be able to use your Sous Vide device to create the most authentic and perfectly cooked Banana oatmeal to start your day on a very energetic note.

Serving: 4

Prep Time: 5 minutes

Cook Time: 6-10 hours

Ingredients:

- 2 cups of rolled oats
- 3 cups of coconut milk
- 3 cups of skimmed milk
- 3 mashed bananas
- 1 teaspoon of vanilla extract

Directions:

1. Set up your Sous Vide immersion cooker to a temperature of 180F and prepare your water bath
2. Add all of the ingredients to your heavy-duty re-sealable zipper bag and seal it up using the water immersion/displacement method
3. Place it under your water bath and let it cook overnight or for about 6-10 hours
4. Once done, pour the oatmeal into serving bowls and add your toppings

Nutritional Info (Per Serving):

- Fat: 25g
- Protein: 19g
- Dietary Fiber: 2g
- Calories: 421

Chocolate and Banana Protein Bites

Forget those expensive and bland tasting protein bites that seamless burn a hole in your pocket! With this Sous Vide recipe, you will be able to create your own protein bites with banana and chocolate.

Serving: 4

Prep Time: 0 minutes

Cook Time: 30 minutes

Ingredients:

- 3 pieces of bananas
- 3 tablespoon of peanut butter
- 3 tablespoon of dark chocolate nibs

Directions:

1. Set up your Sous Vide immersion circulator to a temperature of 140F and prepare your water bath
2. Chop up the bananas into ½ inch slices and add them to a zip bag
3. Add peanut butter, dark chocolate nibs as well
4. Seal using immersion method and cook for 30 minutes
5. Stir the contents and spread it in a popsicle mold
6. Chill and serve!

Nutritional Info (Per Serving):

- Fat: 25g
- Protein: 19g
- Dietary Fiber: 2g
- Calories: 421

Conclusion

THANK YOU!

Dear Friends,

Being a professional cook more than 15 years, I find that it is very important to let you know about that unbelievable healthy modern cooking process and the benefits of using it for your everyday life.

Thank You for getting my Sous Wide cookbook, where I tried to put together my lovely and often used recipes, so hope you will like them and find best ones for you. The recipes are so different that even a younger member of your family can like them.

Hope you will find my cookbook helpful and have it on your kitchen table.

If you have any suggestions I will be very grateful to hear from you in reviews!

Thank You for the interest and Have a Good Day!

Written by: Albert Simon

Copyright © 2018.
All rights reserved.

Made in the USA
San Bernardino, CA
28 June 2018